NANCY KAY'S
ROCKIN' RECIPES

A Collection of Family Favorites

NANCY KAY METZGER

To order additional copies of this book, contact:
Xlibris
1-888-795-4274
www.Xlibris.com
Orders@Xlibris.com

ISBN: Softcover   978-1-7960-9327-8
        Hardcover   978-1-7960-9328-5
        EBook   978-1-7960-9326-1

Print information available on the last page

Rev. date: 03/12/2020

DEDICATION

This cookbook is dedicated to my family and friends who have enjoyed my cooking over the past 50 years. I also dedicate this book to my brother Skip who came up with my nickname "Bette" He started calling me that because he was always amazed that I could put together a wonderful meal when he thought there was nothing to eat in the house.

To him, I WAS his Betty Crocker!

And to all my Facebook friends who have endured my food postings without being able to taste anything...

Sorry for making you all drool! LOL!!!

I hope that you will try these recipes and share them with your family and friends.

...and remember
I LOVE COOKING WITH WINE...
SOMETIMES I EVEN PUT IT IN THE FOOD!
CHEERS...Nancy Kay
AKA "Bette"

Table of Contents

GOTTA HAVE IT!!!

I first got my inspiration to cook at the tender age of 9 when I said to
my mother, Dory, "Mommy, can I make soup?" She didn't hesitate
and asked me what kind of soup did I want to make and
I responded with "what do we have?"

I had a small pot, chicken stock cubes, water and access to whatever was in the fridge. I CUT UP
AND PUT EVERY VEGGIE I COULD FIND INTO MY SOUP plus pasta shells...From that
moment on, in that Eichler kitchen, on my mother's stove in Foster City, CA I fell in love with
cooking and what I could create by just using my imagination and what was in the cupboards...

I have learned over the years that if I don't have a few basic things on hand I couldn't
come up with a new culinary creation when the inspiration struck me and it would
drive me crazy. So as a prologue I would like to outline the 'I gotta have it on hand
at all times" pantry list so my creative cooking soul feels safe and content to cook
or not to cook...Please note that I have not listed how many each recipe serves.
Just think 4 – 6 people and you will have leftovers! I GUARENTEE IT!

HARDWARE
First and foremost ~ really good knives!
~ great pots of all sizes - stainless steel of course
~ tongs, mixing bowls, baking dishes of all kinds
~ A really good dutch oven ~ pizza peel and pan ~ rolling pin

FRESH VEGGIES
I prefer home grown from my garden, of course DUH!!!
~ tomatoes - all kinds, the more the merrier
~ peppers - same thing - all kinds!!!~ red onions ~ scallions
~ shallots ~ carrots ~ celery ~ salad greens ~ cucumbers ~leeks
~ avocados ~ broccoli ~ zucchini ~ artichokes ~ napa cabbage
~ red cabbage

HERBS - FRESH IS BEST
All the fresh herbs you can grow
~ basil ~ oregano ~ thyme ~ lemon thyme ~ sage ~ pineapple sage
~ italian parsley - LOTS n LOTS of this!!! ~ cilantro ~ mint
~ tarragon ~ garlic chives

CANNED/DRIED GOODS
~ canned italian crushed tomatoes ~ jarred pasta sauce
~ canned beans - all kinds~ chicken stock
~ veggie stock ~ beef stock ~ lipton beefy onion soup mix
~ all kinds of pasta ~ flour ~bakers sugar ~ cornmeal
~ baking soda & powder ~ honey ~ yeast

SPICES & OIL
~ kosher salt ~ fresh cracked black pepper
~ really good extra virgin olive oil ~ balsamic vinegar
~ cayenne pepper ~ smoked paprika ~ dried italian herbs ~ chili flakes ~ cumin

FRIDGE ITEMS
~ large jar minced garlic ~ fresh lemons & limes
~ soy sauce ~ eggs ~sour cream ~ butter ~ all kinds of cheese
~ apple chicken sausage ~bacon ~ ground beef ~ ground turkey ~ chicken breasts & thighs

FREEZER ITEMS
~ puffed pastry ~ frozen whole chickens ~ frozen uncooked & cooked prawns

CANNING ITEMS
~ jars & lids ~ canning pot ~ tongs ~ funnel ~ lots of towels

GRILLING ITEMS
~ mesquite charcoal ~ lighter fluid ~ fire starter chimney
~ long tongs ~ grill brush ~ baster brush

STARTERS

CLINKY! ~ CLINKY!

You can bring me ROM anytime! CHEERS!

METZGER MAI TAI

Guaranteed to put a smile on your face and make you wiggle your toes in the sand…Now lay back and enjoy…Aloha baby!!!
~ fill a very tall glass with ice, add
~ 2 shots Bacardi limon rum
~ 2 shots Appleton dark rum
~ 4 shots trader vic's mai tai mix
~ top off with orange pineapple juice to fill the glass
~ stir to blend all flavors
~ add a slice of fresh pineapple
~ add a straw with a little umbrella

MEXICAN MARTINI - Aye Carumba!!

This is an original cocktail invented by me for my boss, Duane Maidens, when I worked at Michael Patrick Partners. Doo really liked this cocktail especially when you garnish it with a doggie dick olive (green olive with a hot chili sticking out of it) - his term, not mine.
~ 2 oz really good tequila - your choice
~ 2 oz fresh lime juice
~ 1 oz triple sec

Fill a cocktail shaker with ice, add ingredients and shakie shakie. Take a chilled martini glass, rub the rim with fresh lime and dip in salt. Pour and garnish with a lime twist wrapped around a hot chili pepper or a doggie dick stuffed hot pepper olive.

THE ULTIMATE SPICY BLOODY MARY

Good any time of day especially with my friend Nancy's Eggs Benedict

~ lots of ice!

~ Lefty O'Doul's Spicy Bloody Mary Mix

~ vodka – DUH!!!

~ creamy hot horseradish

~ Worcestershire, just a dash or two

~ minced garlic, about a teaspoon or more if you like garlic

~ a couple dashes of Tabasco, more if you like a really spicy Bloody!

~ lemon pepper to taste

~ celery stalks – I like the tender ones that are more in the center

~ pickled asparagus – See my recipe in CAN IT! section

~ cocktail onions – Love, Love, Love these guys!!!

~ olives - stuffed or not your choice, I like the blue cheese ones

~ pickled artichokes

~ pickled veggies

~ lemon or lime, I prefer lemon!

Rub the rim of your glass with lime or lemon and dip in salt. Fill glasses with lots of ice. Add your Vodka according to how strong you want it. Add horseradish, garlic, tabasco and lemon pepper to taste. Stir to mix well. Add celery stalk & pickled asparagus to the glass. It's time to assemble the rest of the garnish. Take a wooden skewer and use the photo as an inspiration! You can do no wrong here. Another nice touch is to add grilled prawns. It's a meal in a glass. SO YUMMY!!!

BITE ME!

GUACK-TASTIC!
Voted best guacamole on the planet, according to Bay Area locals
~ 6 avacodos – cubed and slightly mashed but still chunky
~ 2 packages quacamole seasoning mix (1 mild, 1 spicy)
~ juice of one lime
~ 1 shallot minced
~ minced garlic to taste
~ 1 tablespoons medium hot salsa salsa
~ salt & pepper to taste

Combine all ingredients in a medium bowl, mix well but leave some chuncks of avocado. Cover with plastic and chill for at least an hour. Put Guack in a festive bowl and top with chopped cilantro. Serve with blue corn tortilla chips. Always a standard go to when friends drop by.

DEVILISH DEVILED EGGS
My mother used to make these all the time when I was a kid. Of course I added to her recipe to make it my own. These ain't Dory's deviled eggs any more!
~ 6 extra large eggs
~ 1-2 tablespoons dijon mustard
~ 1-2 tablespoons mayo
~ 1 shallot, minced
~ 1 stalk minced celery, I use the tender stalks that are in the middle
~ minced garlic
~ a dash of hot sauce
~ salt & pepper to taste
~ paprika
~ cooked bacon (2 – 3 slices) crumbled
~ 1 tablespoon chopped italian parsley

Hard boil the eggs and cool completely. Cook the bacon, drain on paper towel and crumble after it has cooled. Cut the eggs in half and put the yokes in a medium bowl, place egg halves on a serving platter. Add all ingredients except the bacon crumbles, Italian parsley & paprika to the yolk mixture, mix well. Add salt & pepper to taste. Fill each egg half with a generous amount of the yolk mixture. Sprinkle with paprika, add bacon crumbles & chopped parsley. Happy hour happiness.

CHEESY PINWHEELS

Because what is better than lots of cheese baked with buttery pastry in little pinwheels shapes?

~ 1 package puff pastry
~ 1 cup asiago cheese, shredded
~ 1 cup extra sharp chedder cheese, shredded
~ fresh chopped italian parsley & basil

Preheat oven to 350. Defrost the puff pastry. Grate the cheese. Layout the pastry sheet and cover with the cheese herb mixture. Roll up into a log sealing the end with a little water. Wrap in plastic wrap and chill for 30 minutes. Slice into pinwheels and place on a cookie sheet and bake for about 15 minutes or until they are golden brown.

This is a great Happy Hour munch.

SLURP!

ROASTED RED PEPPER SOUP

This is my former mother-in-laws favorite! Original recipe is from Fresco's restaurant in Palo Alto, which no longer exists. Traditionally, I make this every December for family & friends just because I CAN!!!

~ 12 jars (15 oz) roasted red peppers
~ 2 red onion, chopped
~ 2 yellow onion, chopped
~ minced garlic to taste
~ 1 stick of butter
~ 2 boxes chicken stock
~ 1 large jar garlic lovers salsa
~ salt & lemon pepper to taste

Melt butter is large stock pot. add onions and saute until translucent. Add the other ingredients, bring to a boil and cook for 15 - 20 minutes. Puree the soup mixture in a food processor until smooth. Serve with cheesy garlic bread and fuji apple salad.

CHICKEN WILD RICE SOUP

This is my favorite soup to make when anyone I know is sick (except for my vegan friends of course). I also make this without the rice and use it when I'm trying to loose weight. Great flavor, great protien and little calories, NICE!!!!

~ olive oil
~ 1 package boneless, skinles chicken breasts, cubed
~ minced garlic to taste
~ 1 red onion, rough chopped
~ 5 stalks celery, rough chopped
~ 2-3 boxes chicken stock
~ 1 can white corn
~ 5 small red, yellow & orange peppers diced

~ 10 small baby carrots cut into bite size pieces
~ 2 can italian style crushed tomatoes
~ 2 zuchinni, halved then diced
~ 1 pound mushrooms, sliced
~ 2 leeks halved then sliced
~ ADD ANY OTHER VEGGIES YOU LIKE!!!
~ 1 box wild rice

Put olive oil in a large soup pot. Add onion and garlic and saute until translucent. Add chicken and continue to saute until chicken is cooked through. Add stock. Add all other ingredients and simmer until the rice is cooked, about an hour. Server with crusty sourdough bread.

GARDEN GASPACHO WITH BABY SHRIMP
Yes, I use all my garden veggies for this one. Why go to the store when you can shop in your own backyard???
~ 10 fresh tomatoes from the garden, skinned and chopped
~ 1 large fresh cucumber, peeled & chopped
~ 1 bunch of green onions, chopped
~ 1 zucchini, chopped
~ 1 can Mexican style stewed tomatoes
~ 1 bottle spicy V-8 juice
~ 1 pound cooked baby shrimp
~ salt & lemon peper to taste
~ fresh cilantro

Combine all ingredients in a large bowl. Cover and chill for at least 1 hour. Top with some guack and cilantro and serve.

4 ONION SOUP

Who doesn't love French Onion soup? I just took it to a whole new level!!!

~ 2 sticks butter

~ minced garlic to taste

~ 2 red onions

~ 2 yellow onions

~ 2 white onions

~ 2 walla walla onions

~ 2 boxes beef stock

~ 4 cans consommé

~ sourdough provolone cheesy bread

All onions should be cut in half and thinly sliced. Melt butter in large stock pot, add garlic and onions. Cook down until translucent. Add stock and consommé simmer for 30 minutes or more. In a toaster oven or broiler place sourdough slices topped with provolone cheese and toast until melted. Fill bowls with soup and top with cheesy bread.

BEAN & BACON SOUP

Just had to figure how to make this from scratch...hate Campbell's condensed soup!!!

~ olive oil

~ minced garlic to taste

~ 4 stalk celery, diced

~ 1 red onion, diced

~ 3 carrots, diced

~ 2 cans white beans

~ 2 cans pinto beans

~ 2 cans black beans

~ 2 boxes chicken stock

~ 1-pound bacon, cut up and cooked

~ crushed saltine crackers as topping

Cover bottom of stock pot with olive oil. Over medium heat cook garlic, celery, onion & carrots until translucent. Add all cans of beans. Mix well.

Add enough chicken stock to cover the bean mixture. Bring to a boil then simmer for an hour. While the beans are simmering, cut up and cook bacon. drain fat then add cooked bacon to soup. Simmer for at least 30 more minutes. The more you simmer the soup the better the flavor will be. It will get thicker the longer you cook it so feel free to add more chicken stock if you feel it is getting too thick. The soup is really good with crushed saltine crackers used as a topping; you can leave off if you are not a saltine fan.

ITALIAN WHITE BEAN SOUP WITH MUSHROOMS

Another family favorite…I just made this up one afternoon. My Dad loved this soup. I used to make it and freeze it in seal a meal bags and Fed Ex it to him in Scottsdale. Yummy and good for you too.

~2 pounds Italian season ground turkey

~ 4 bags sliced white mushrooms

~ 1 large red onion

~ minced garlic to taste

~ 4 cans cannellini beans

~ 1 large can crushed italian seasoned tomatoes

~ 1 big bunch of Italian parsley

~ chicken stock as needed

~ olive oil

~ salt & pepper to taste

In a large pot add oil and heat up. Add onion and mushrooms and cook down until just soft. Remove onion/mushroom mixture from pot. Add more oil and brown the ground turkey. Add back the veggies. Add beans, crushed tomatoes and chopped parsley. Mix well and bring to a boil then turn it down to simmer. If it seems too thick add some broth if not, then leave it alone. Simmer for about an hour and serve with crusty sourdough bread.

SEAFOOD CIOPPINO

This a such a fun and healthy meal to make for a large gathering.

~ 3 tablespoons olive oil

~ 1 red onion, chopped

~ 3 large shallots, minced

~ minced garlic to taste

~ red pepper flakes to taste

~ 1 small can tomato paste

~ 2 cans crushed italian tomatoes

~ 1 ¼ cup white wine

~ 5 cups fish or veggie stock

~ a couple bay leaves

~ salt & pepper to taste

~ 1-pound clams

~ 1-pound mussels

~ 1-pound large shrimp, peeled and deveined

~ 1-pound large sea scallops

~ 1 cracked dungeness crab

Heat the olive oil in a Dutch oven over medium heat. Add chopped onions and shallots and season with salt. Sauté until the onions & shallots are translucent. Add garlic and red chili flakes. Sauté for another 2 minutes. Add tomato paste and crushed Italian tomatoes. Stir well. Next add wine, fish stock and bay leaf. Bring to a simmer and cover. Reduce heat to medium low and simmer until the flavors blend, approximately 30 minutes stirring occasionally. Add the clams and mussels, cover again and simmer until the clams and mussels open. About 5 minutes. Next into the pot add the shrimp, scallops and crab. Simmer gently until they are cooked through and the clams & mussels are completely open. Discard any clams or mussels that did not open. You DO NOT want to eat those! Season to taste and serve it up with my cheesy garlic bread!

CRUNCH!

FUJI APPLE, WALNUT AND BLUE CHEESE SALAD WITH BALSAMIC VINAIGRETTE DRESSING
House favorite!!! I just love this salad. The sweet crunch of the Fuji apple, the tang of the dressing and the bite of the blue cheese!
~ 1 bunch romaine lettuce, rough chopped
~ 1 fuji apple, cored and chopped
~ 1 cup regular walnuts or glazed walnuts, rough chopped
~ 1 cup crumbled blue cheese
~ balsamic vinaigrette dressing
(3 tablespoons balsamic vinegar, 1 tablespoon dijon mustard, 1 small clove minced garlic, 1 tsp minced shallot, pinch of dried thyme, 1/3c extra virgin olive oil)

Combine all ingredients except dressing in a large salad bowl, toss to mix well. Add dressing just before serving. Goes great with everything!

COLD ARTICHOKE STUFFED WITH SHRIMP SALAD
This is a re-creation of a salad that we used to serve at the Skywood Grill (aka Skywood Chateau) back in the day...Another restaurant that is no longer around but the salad lives on through me!
~ 2 steamed artichokes
~ 1 cup sourdough bread cubes
~ 1 shallot, minced
~ minced garlic to taste
~ 1 stalk celery, minced
~ 1 tablespoon chopped italian parsley
~ 1 cup cooked baby shrimp
~ balsamic vinaigrette dressing
~ salt & lemon pepper to taste

Cook and chill the artichokes. Clean out middle to create a "cup to hold the salad. In a medium bowl combine all ingredients except the dressing. Mix well then add just enough dressing to moisten the bread cubes so that the "salad" holds together. Fill the artichokes with the shrimp salad and chill until ready to serve. Add chilled grilled prawns as an extra topping.

COLD COOS COOS VEGGIE SALAD

This is a great summer salad to serve at your next BBQ

~ 1 box reqular coos coos
~ 1 can garbanzo beans
~ 3 sweet peppers, red, yellow & orange
~ 1 medium shallot minced
~ 1 celery stock, minced
~ 1/2 peeled and seeded cucumber, diced into bite size pieces
~ minced garlic to taste
~ salt & pepper
~ lemon herb vinaigrette dressing – see recipe under Mediterranean pasta salad
~ 1/2 cup mix of chopped mint and italian parsley

Make coos coos according to package directions, put in fridge and let it chill out. Dice up all veggies but don't make them too small, you want them to "pop" in this salad but not too big to overpower the coos coos. Mix the coos coos with the veggies, garlic and 1/2 the chopped herbs in a large serving bowl. Drizzle with the vinaigrette, mix well then add salt and pepper to taste. Garnish with remaing chopped herbs and serve with BBQ'd leg of lamb.

SWEET VEGGIE SALAD

This recipe comes from Hale Sr's Narna, Grace ,Jean Deady, I just added the jicama for a little extra crunch :)

~ 1 can small sweet peas
~ 2 cans cut green beans
~ 1 can baby corn
~ 1 cup roasted red pepper, diced

~ 1 large red onion, chopped
~ 1 medium jicama, peeled and chopped
~ 1 cup sugar
~ 1 cup vinegar
~ 1/2 cup canola oil
~ salt & pepper to taste

Put all veggie ingredients in a large bowl. Toss to mix. In a small sauce pan heat sugar, vinegar, & oil until dissolved. Pour dressing over veggie mix, cover and refrigerate ovenight.

MEDITERRANEAN PASTA SALAD
This makes a fantastic potluck salad.
~ 1 box bow tie pasta
~ 1 english cucumber, peeled and diced
~ 2/3 cup sliced kalamata olives
~ 4 ounces crumbled feta cheese
~ half of a medium red onion, peeled and thinly sliced

LEMON HERB VINAIGRETTE
~ 1/4 cup extra virgin olive oil
~ 3 tablespoons balsamic vinegar
~ 1 tablespoon freshly squeezed lemon juice
~ 2 teaspoons fresh oregano, minced
~ 1 teaspoon honey *(or your desired sweetener)*
~ minced garlic to taste
~ salt and freshly cracked black pepper to taste
~ pinch of crushed red pepper flakes, to taste
~ whisk all ingredients until combined

Cook the pasta al dente in a large stockpot of salted water according to package instructions. Drain pasta, then rinse under cold water for about 20-30 seconds until cool. Put the pasta in a large mixing bowl. Add cucumber, tomatoes, kalamata olives, feta cheese, and red onion to the pasta then drizzle the vinaigrette evenly on top. Toss until all of the ingredients are evenly coated with the dressing. Serve immediately, garnished with extra feta and black pepper if desired. This goes really well with my BBQ bourbon wings also a great picnic salad.

FRENCH POTATO SALAD

I love this recipe because it does not have mayonnaise and I just love the firmness of the smaller red potatoes. The lemon Dijon dressing is very light and refreshing. Great for a picnic on a boat on the Bay. Trust me I've done it and the Captain was very impressed with his First Mate!

~ 3 pounds red potatoes, cubed

~ 1/3 cup olive oil

~ juice of 1 freshly squeezed lemon

~ minced garlic to taste

~ 1 shallot, minced

~ 2 teaspoons Dijon mustard

~ salt & lemon pepper to taste

~ finely chopped fresh herbs *(rosemary, chives, tarragon, thyme, dill, and italian parsley)*

Place the diced potatoes in a large stockpot and add enough water so that the potatoes are covered by 1 inch. Cook over medium-high heat until the water reaches a boil. Then reduce heat to medium to simmer and continue cooking the potatoes until they pierce easily with a fork. Drain the potatoes in a colander and place in the fridge for 20-30 minutes. In the meantime, while the potatoes are chillin', whisk together the olive oil, lemon juice, garlic, mustard, salt and lemon pepper in a bowl. Once the potatoes are chilled combine them in a large serving bowl with the dressing, shallot and fresh herbs. Toss gently to combine. Add more salt & lemon pepper if needed. Cover and refrigerate for 1-2 hours. This goes really well with my BBQ Bourbon Wings.

THE MAIN EVENT

These dishes are for many like 4 to 6, not just 1 or 2. If you have a small family please share with your neighbors, as I do. They may not mow your lawn or take in your mail when you are on vacation but they will thank you and always show up when the wonderful smell of your cooking travels down wind to their doorway....

MAMA MIA

LA – SAG – NA

(pronounced just as I have spelled it) a tribute to Bill Puchinelli, the man who started to Blue Fox restaurant in San Francisco back in the day and also took out his teeth to entertain us all whenever he could when we were kids. Be warned this is a 2-day event! Home canned tomato sauce is best and so totally worth the effort. If not, then go buy jar Marinara at the store and move on.

DAY ONE – THE SAUCE
~ olive oil
~ minced garlic, as much as you want baby. The more the merrier for me! It's good for your heart, why do you think Italians live so long?
~ 2 red onions chopped
~ 2 pounds premium ground beef
~ 2 pounds mild Italian sausage
~ 4 cans italian stewed tomatoes
~ 1 family size spaghetti sauce mix
~ 2 cups water
~ 1 can tomato paste
~ 1 bunch fresh italian parsley, chopped
~ 1 bunch fresh basil, chopped
~ 1 bunch oregano, chopped
~ salt & pepper to taste

Add olive oil to a 5-quart soup pot. Saute garlic & onion until translucent. Add beef and sausage, cook completely. Add stewed tomatoes, spaghetti sauce mix, tomato paste, water and herbs. stir to combine. Simmer all day stirring occasionaly being careful to keep the sauce at the bottom of the pan from burning.

DAY TWO - THE ASSEMBLY
~ sauce from the day before
~ 2 boxes no bake lasagna noodles
~ 2 pounds mozzarella cheese, grated
~ 2 pounds ricotta cheese
~ 4 large zucchinis, grated
~ 1 cup grated parmesan cheese

Preheat oven to 350 degrees. These noodles do not need to be precooked. They will cook in the sauce as the lasagna bakes. Layer the ingredients in a large deep lasagna pan as follows. First put sauce in the bottom of the dish then put a layer of noodles. Add sauce, mozzarella, zucchini and then ricotta, start again with the noodle layer and continue on until the pan is full. Finish with sauce and then top with the parmesan cheese. Bake for approx. 1 hour. Serve with your choice of salad.

BOW TIE PASTA WITH CHICKEN APPLE SAUSAGE

This is the beautiful Miss Kela's favorite dinner
and oh so easy to make. She loves her bow tie pasta!

~ olive oil

~ 1 package chicken apple sausage

~ 1 small red onion

~ minced garlic to taste

~ 1 to 2 jars store or homemade marinara sauce

~ 1 box bow tie pasta

Heat up olive oil in medium saute pan, brown sausage, onion & garlic until onions caramelize and the sausage is brown. Add sauce to pan and heat through. In a separate pot boil water and add salt, cook pasta. When pasta is al dente drain and return to stock pot. Pour sausage sauce over the pasta and toss to mix well. Serve with salad and cheesy garlic bread.

MAC N CHESSE BACON CUPS

Kela and I made this one up one Saturday afternoon so she would have snack in the freezer for lunch when she started her new job. So very proud of her!

~ 4 slices of crispy bacon (or more if you like)

~ 2 cups elbows pasta or any type that you like

~ 2 tablespoons panko

~ 2 tablespoons freshly grated parmesan

~ 1 1/2 teaspoons olive oil

~ 2 tablespoons unsalted butter

~ minced garlic to taste

~ 2 tablespoons all-purpose flour

~ 1 cup milk

~ 1 cup sour cream

~ 2 cups shredded extra sharp cheddar cheese – tillamook is the house favorite
~ 1 large egg, beaten
~ salt and pepper, to taste
~ 1 tablespoon chopped fresh chives or italian parsley for topping

Preheat oven to 425. Line a 12-cup standard muffin tin with paper liners or coat with nonstick spray, I like to use the oversized muffin tins. More bang for your buck! In a large pot of boiling salted water, cook pasta according to package instructions; drain well. To make topping, combine panko, parmesan and olive together. Melt butter in a large saucepan over medium heat. Add garlic, and cook, stirring frequently, until fragrant, about 1-2 minutes. Whisk in flour until lightly browned, about 1 minute. Gradually whisk in milk and sour cream. Bring to a boil; reduce heat and simmer, whisking constantly, until thickened, about 3-5 minutes. Remove from heat. Stir in cheese until melted. Pour the cheese sauce into a large mixing bowl. Add pasta and bacon. Gently toss to combine, stir in egg and mix well. Season with salt and pepper, to taste. Scoop the pasta mixture evenly into the muffin tray. Sprinkle with panko cheese topping. Into the oven it goes and bakes for 18-20 minutes, or until golden brown. Serve immediately, garnished with chives or rough chopped Italian parsley. If you want to save them for later, let them cool and put in freezer bags and freeze them and take them out as needed. This is what Kela and I did so she had food in her freezer. Thaw and reheat in the oven. Do not microwave them they DO NOT hold up to the Microwaving process. We will be making these again soon. Such a great Mother/Daughter cooking day!

LINGUINE AND CLAMS IN WHITE WINE SAUCE

This is a great date night meal. You should try this out on your honey and see what happens next!

~ 1 package fresh linguini

~ a dozen or so clams

~ 2 tablespoons butter

~ olive oil

~ minced garlic to taste

~ a package of frozen clam meat

~ 1 bottle clam juice

~ 1 cup white wine

~ red pepper flakes, to taste

~ salt & lemon pepper to taste (see there is that lemon thing again)

~ juice of 1 fresh lemon (more lemon, I'm in heaven!)

~ chopped italian parsley

~ chopped basil

~ chopped oregano

~ grated parmesan cheese

Add olive oil to a heavy Dutch oven and heat. Once the oil is hot you can add the minced garlic and cook until light brown. Add the clams and wine & clam juice. Cover and cook until the clams start to open. About 10 minutes. Discard any clams that did not open! Remove the clams from the pan and set aside. Add more oil and add a bit more garlic and red pepper flakes (to your taste), add defrosted package of clam meat. Add a little more wine and cover to simmer while you cook the pasta. Fill a large pot with salted water and bring to a boil. Check in on your clams before dropping the pasta. Since it is fresh it won't take that long to cook. You want it to be al dente! Once the pasta is done add the butter to the clam mix. Stir until it has completely melted. Once the pasta is done, drain it and add it to the clams. Add fresh herbs and mix completely so the pasta is covered with the clam mixture. Add the cheese and mix well. The cheese will thicken the sauce. Once that is all mixed together you can add back in the clams in their shells to warm them. Serve in big bowls with more cheese and herbs and a squeeze of fresh lemon. Serve with a mixed greens salad with balsamic vinaigrette or wedge salad with blue cheese dressing.

LINGUINE WITH LEMON SAUCE

I am a sucker for anything that has a lemon sauce, but you probably figured that out by now!

~ 1 package fresh linguine

~ 2 tablespoons butter

~ 1 tablespoon freshly grated lemon zest, plus more for serving

~ 2 tablespoons freshly squeezed lemon juice

~ 4 tablespoons heavy cream

~ 2 tablespoons freshly grated parmesan cheese

~ 1 bunch italian parsley, pull leaves off the stems to garnish

~ extra cheese to serve on the side, you can never have too much cheese!

Bring a pot of salted water to boil. Heat the butter in a skillet and add the lemon zest. Drop the linguine into the boiling water. Cook pasta according to package directions. Drain. Add the cream to the butter and lemon zest mixture. Add the pasta and lemon juice and stir until just heated through. Add the parmesan and toss. Serve with additional parmesan and lemon zest on the side. Garnish with pulled italian parsley leaves.

VOLCANO PIZZA!

Watch out Round Table I'm a coming for you!!

Thus named for the way the crust is formed around it's molten hot cheesy center...A very unique presentation. My kids LOVE this.

~ 3 1/2 cups flour

~ 1 cup warm water

~ 2 tablespoons yeast

~ 1/4 cup olive oil

~ 2 tablespoon's honey

~ 1/2 teaspoon salt

~ corn meal

~ whatever toppings you want (see picture above for some ideas)

Put all dough ingredients in a bread maker and set to "dough" setting and hit start. The machine will do the work and when it beeps you are ready to make pizza. Preheat your oven to

the hottest setting with the pizza stone on the middle rack. Prepare your toppings while the dough is doughing. Use whatever you like. Jarred sauce is just fine. Layer your ingredients. Sauce, cheese, filling and then another layer. Top with cheese and pull the dough up around the filling until it looks like the picture. Make sure that you have a pizza peel, corn meal and a pizza stone then you

are good to go! Put corn meal on the pizza peel before you put the dough on the peel and then just layer. Slide off pizza onto pre heated pizza stone and bake until it looks like the picture below. Timing will depend on your oven temp. Mine is usually 15 to 20 minutes. Just keep an eye on it and don't let it get away from you! You will use the pizza peel to get it out of the oven. Place on a wire rack to "settle" about 10 – 15 minutes or else if you cut into it right away you will have one cheesy mess! I usually cut this into quarters. 1 quarter per serving and you will need a fork!

See it looks like a volcano!

MOOOOO...

BEST DAMN MEATLOAF EVER

Yes, it really, really is!

~ 2 lbs lean ground beef

~ 1 lb ground pork

~ 1 lb ground veal or turkey

~ 1 chopped red onion

~ minced garlic to taste

~ 2 envelopes lipton onion & mushroom soup mix

~ 1 cup garlic & herb breadcrumbs

~ 1 cup italian seasoned breadcrumbs

~ 2 eggs

~ 1/3 cup each of catchup, A1 sauce & BBQ sauce

~ 1/2 cup water

~ salt & pepper to taste

~ 1 jar roasted garlic pasta sauce

Preheat oven to 350. Mix all ingredients together until they are totally incorporated. Form loaf in large baking dish. Pour pasta sauce over loaf. Bake 1 hour or until done. Serve with garlic smashed potatoes & fuji apple & blue cheese salad

NANCY'S QUICK POT ROAST

Seriously this is the quick version. Come home at 6pm and it's ready to eat at 8pm. Of course it's always way better the next day!

~ 4 – 5 lb chuck roast, salt & pepper before cooking
~ olive oil
~ minced garlic to taste
~ 1 box lipton onion & mushroom soup mix
~ 1 red onion, chopped
~ 1 bunch celery
~ 6 red potatoes
~ 1 small bag baby peeled carrots
~ 1 bag sliced mushrooms

Heat pan and add olive oil & garlic. Brown meat for about 5 minutes on each side. Add enough water to fully cover the meat. Add chopped onion.

Add 2 packets lipton onion & mushroom soup mix. Boil on medium high heat for 2 – 3 hours. When meat starts to fall apart add the remaining veggies and simmer until done. If you want a thicker sauce, add 3 – 4 tablespoons wondra gravy flour dissolved in warm water. Serve with crusty sourdough bread and butter.

BEEF STEW

Your basic stew. It should cook all day.The longer it cooks the better it gets!

~ olive oil

~ 2 pounds stew meat - bite size pieces dredged in flour

~ 1 red onion

~ minced garlic to taste

~ 2-3 boxes beef stock

~ 1 bunch celery, chopped

~ 1 bag baby carrots

~ 6 medium red potatoes, cubed

~ salt & pepper to taste

Heat olive oil in a large pot. Add beef and brown. Remove from pot and add more oil cook onion & garlic until translucent. Add beef back to the pot along with stock and bring to a boil. Let simmer for 2 hours then add the carrots and celery. The potatoes should be added about a half an hour before serving. This stew always pairs well with crusty sourdough bread.

BUZZIE'S BLUE CHEESEBURGERS

My Dad used to make these. It is such a flavor explosion on your mouth. Serve on toasted Ciabatta rolls. YUM!

~ 1 pound premium ground beef

~ 1 tablespoon Worceshire sause

~ 1 packet onion soup mix

~ crumbled blue cheese

~ ciabatta rolls

Mix beef, Worcshire and onion soup mix together. I like to use my hands so it really gets mixed well. Take 1/2 mixture roll it into a ball then make a hole is it. Stuff the hole with blue cheese and close the hole. flatten into patty. I like to bbq them but you can cook then in a pan on the stove.

Toast the buns either on the grill or in a toaster oven. Serve with whatever condiments you like. A good side dish would be my sweet veggie salad.

HERB CRUSTED CROSS RIB ROAST

This one is easy. Get a good-sized cross rib roast, put it on a roasting rack in your roasting pan then coat with the following mixture

HERB CRUST
~ 1/2 c olive oil
~ lots of minced garlic
~ 1 tablespoons Dijon mustard
~ fresh rosemary, thyme, italian parsley & oregano - as much as you want, I like more as you can see from the picture :)
~ kosher salt
~ fresh crack black pepper

Preheat oven to 350. In a medium bowl mix the olive oil, mustard, garlic and fresh chopped herbs. Add salt & pepper to taste. Mix well. Rub all over the roast and let it sit for 30 minutes before you put in the oven. Cook roast for the standard rule of 20 minutes per pound. Serve with garlic smashed potatoes and fuji apple salad.

BRAISED SHORT RIBS

This is a great meal for a chilly fall day

~ 5-pound bone-in beef short ribs cut crosswise into 2» pieces

~ salt and pepper

~ all-purpose flour for dredging

~ 3 tablespoons olive oil

~ 3 medium onions chopped

~ 3 medium carrots chopped

~ 2 celery stalks chopped

~ 3 tablespoons all-purpose flour

~ 1 tablespoon tomato paste

~ 1 bottle dry red wine preferably cabernet Sauvignon

~ 10 sprigs italian parsley

~ 8 sprigs thyme

~ 4 sprigs oregano

~ 2 sprigs rosemary

~ 2 fresh or dried bay leaves

~ 2 heads of garlic halved crosswise

~ 4 cups beef stock

MASH

~ 3 pounds yukon gold potatoes

~ 8 tablespoons heavy cream

~ 3 tablespoons butter

~ 4 tablespoons shredded parmesan cheese

~ 4 tablespoons sour cream

~ salt and pepper to taste

~ freshly chopped chives

Preheat oven to 350. Season short ribs liberally with salt and pepper. Dredge in flour to cover all sides. Heat oil in a large Dutch oven over medium-high heat. Working in 2 batches, brown short ribs on all sides. Take browned ribs out of pot and set aside. Add onions, carrots, and celery to pot and cook over medium-high heat, stirring often, until onions are browned. Add flour and tomato paste until well combined and deep red. Stir in wine, then add short ribs. Bring to a boil and reduce heat to medium and simmer until wine is reduced by half. Add all herbs to pot along with garlic. Stir in stock. Bring to a boil, cover, and transfer to oven. Cook until short ribs are tender, 2 - 2 1/2 hours. Place short ribs on a platter. Strain sauce from pot into a bowl. Remove any fat from surface and season to taste with salt and pepper. You should be prepping your mash while the ribs are in the oven. Peel and cube potatoes. Cut into quarters. Place in a large pot and cover with water. Bring to a boil and then reduce heat to medium low to maintain a rolling boil. Cook until potatoes until you can easily pierce them with a fork. When potatoes are ready remove from heat and drain. Put them back into the warm pot. Add the cream, butter, sour cream and Parmesan, and MASH with a potato masher. Season with salt and pepper and fold in the chopped chives. Serve in shallow bowls by adding MASH to the bottom of the bowls, place 1 – 2 ribs on top of MASH and spoon sauce over that. Garnish with chopped fresh herbs. Your choice.

SAUCY MEAT BALLS

When I couldn't find ground veal at the store, I substituted ground turkey. If you can get the Italian seasoned variety, it adds more flavor!!

~ 2 lbs lean ground beef

~ 1 pound ground pork

~ 1 pound ground turkey

~ 1 package sliced mushrooms

~ 3 chopped shallots

~ minced garlic to taste

~ 2 envelopes lipton onion & mushroom soup mix

~ 2 cups garlic & herb bread crumbs

~ 4 eggs

~ 1/3 cup each of catchup, A1 sauce & BBQ sauce

~ 1/2 cup water

~ 1 bag Italian mix cheese

~ 1 bunch fresh italian parsley, chopped

~ 1 bunch fresh basil, chopped

~ salt & pepper to taste

~ 2 jars roasted garlic pasta sauce. Or your own canned sauce. Of course, I use MINE! You want them to be really saucy!

In a saucepan add olive oil and butter. Add the chopped-up mushrooms & shallots. Sauté until translucent. Remove from heat and set aside. Next up is to mix your meats together. Best done is a large bowl using your hands. Add Lipton Soup mix and mix well again. Next add the breadcrumbs, mix again. Add catchup, A1 and BBQ sauce, mixed again and add the eggs. Mix well again. Add the mushrooms and shallot mixture, Mix again. Last in the pool are the fresh herbs and red pepper flakes if you like a little heat in your meatballs. That's a SPICY MEATBALL!! Don't forget to add the cheeses to the meat mixture, Again, mix well then make into balls. I make mine on the larger size, a little smaller than a tennis ball and bigger than a golf ball. You make them whatever size you'd like! Brown them all on a sauté pan before putting in a baking dish. Once in the baking dish cover with all the sauce and bake at 350 for an hour. Remove from oven and serve over your favorite pasta. Or just by themselves. They don't need no stinking pasta!

NANCY'S ROCKIN' SPICY BOURBON BEEF JERKY

I was hesitant to include this recipe as I have guarded it from anyone having it for quite some time. It's not that hard to make but there are a lot of ingredients and I usually GO BIG making at least 15 pounds of Jerky at a time. This recipe is enough for 5 pounds of jerky.

~ 5 pounds of london broil
~ 1 cup balsamic vinegar

~ 1 cup apple cider
~ 1 cup soy sauce
~ 1 cup Worcestershire
~ 2 tbsp liquid smoke
~ 1 cup bourbon
~ ¼ cup dijon mustard
~ ¼ cup unpasteurized honey
~ 3 tablespoons garlic powder
~ 3 tablespoons onion powder
~ 2 dried chipotle chiles chopped

~ 1 cup brown sugar
~ 3 tablespoons sesame oil
~ ¼ teaspoon ground clove
~ 2 tablespoons smoked paprika
~ minced garlic and lots of it!
~ 2 tablespoons crushed chili pepper

First step is to make the marinade. Super simple. Just measure and combine everything in a large pot that has a lid. Stir to mix well and be sure the brown sugar is dissolved. Next up preparing the meat. You'll want to partially freeze it as it will make cutting it so much easier. Use a serrated knife to cut into your jerky strips. Once cut place the meat in the marinade. Cover and let set in the fridge for 3 days stirring occasionally to be sure all strips are getting the full marinade love! Final step is drying it. You will need cookie baking sheets and wire racks. Put the rack on the baking sheet and lay the meat on it a single layer on each sheet. The oven will be on its lowest setting. Place the racks in the oven and "forget about it" for at least 6 hours. You can check on them after that. If you feel they have dried properly then you are done, if not, leave them in longer. Once you are satisfied that the are done you can take them out to cool and then put into plastic bags. It should keep pretty well for about a month. Longer if you use a food saver and seal them in vacuum bags. This is what I do as I make so much and give it to my friends and family. Now you can too!

BAC, BAC, BAC
Super Chicken!

CHICKEN ROLL UPS

I just made this up one night. Pretty awesome...
Great for a dinner party!

~ 4 chicken breasts, skin/boneless
~ 2 - 3 tablespoons olive oil
~ minced garlic to taste
~ 1 red onion, diced
~ 1 pound brown mushrooms, sliced
~ 1/2 lb fresh baby spinach leaves, washed
~ 2 cups ricotta cheese
~ 1 cup parmesan cheese, grated
~ 1 cup asiago cheese, grated
~ salt & pepper to taste
~ 28 oz can italian style crushed tomatoes
~ 1 cup mozzarella cheese, grated

Preheat oven to 350. Pound chicken breasts until 1/4" thick, Set aside. Add olive oil to a large sauté pan and heat. When the olive oil is hot, add garlic, onions & mushrooms. Sauté until soft. Remove from heat and set aside to cool. Put ricotta cheese in blender, add mushroom/onion mixture and blend. Sprinkle cutting board with flour, lay pounded chicken breast on board and spread chicken with cheese mixture. Top cheese layer with baby spinach leaves. Roll up chicken breast and place in baking dish. Repeat process until all of the chicken breasts are rolled and in the baking dish. Season with salt and pepper. Cover with crushed tomatoes and top with grated mozzarella cheese. Bake at 350 for 1 hour. Serve with salad and sourdough bread.

CHICKEN IN PUFFED PASTRY WITH DIJON CREAM SAUCE

a Bette original!

~ 1 box puff pastry sheets (2 per box), defrosted in fridge

~ 2 skin less boneless chicken breasts cut into bite size pieces

~ stuffing mix, homemade or store bought

~ 1 bag white mushrooms

~ 2 medium shallots finely minced

~ 2 tablespoons olive oil

~ 1 tablespoon butter

~ ½ white wine

~ 2 tablespoons dijon mustard

~ 2 tablespoons chopped parsley & thyme

~ minced garlic to taste

~1/2 cup heavy cream

~ salt and pepper to taste

Preheat oven to 400. Next finely chop the mushrooms and shallots. Heat a large skillet to medium heat and add olive oil. Add the butter and once its melted add the mushrooms, shallots and garlic. Cook until softened. Remove and set aside. Add more olive oil. Add chicken bites and cook until tender. Do not overcook them as they will become tough and not pleasant at all. Once done remove chicken from skillet and add to stuffing mix in a large bowl. Next add the mushroom mixture to the stuffing. Stir well to combine. Add chicken stock as needed to make the stuffing mix moist but not soggy! Time for the puff pastry. Unfold and cut each sheet into 4 squares. You can roll them out a bit but not too much or they won't puff! Place filling in the center of each square, brush edges with a little water and pinch corners at the top and crimp the sides to make a little pillow. In a baking dish spread a layer of olive oil and place the pillows in the dish. Once the oven is ready bake the pillows for about 15 minutes or until they have puffed and are golden brown. Time for the dijon cream sauce! In the skillet that you used previously deglaze the pan with white wine over medium heat. Add heavy cream and dijon mustard with the herbs. Salt & pepper to taste. Bring to a simmer and reduce by half and the sauce has thickened. Once the sauce is ready you can plate your chicken in puff pastry and drizzle the dijon cream sauce over the top and around the sides of the plate. Serve with salad or all by itself.

AWESOME 4 BEAN TURKEY CHILI

Not a Texas style chili by a long shot but really really good! My Mom used to make a mid-western version, so I thought I'd change it up adding different types of beans and white corn.

~ olive oil
~ 2 pounds premium ground turkey meat
~ 1 box Shelly chili mix
~ 1 large red onion, chopped
~ 4 cans Mexican style stewed tomatoes
~ 2 cans black beans
~ 2 cans chili beans
~ 2 cans pinto beans
~ 2 cans white beans
~ 1 can white corn
~ salt & pepper to taste

Heat olive oil in a large stock pot. Sauté onion until translucent. Add turkey and cook though. Add seasoning packet from the chili mix. Add tomatoes, beans and corn including the juice from the cans. Add cayenne pepper packet if you want some kick, if not, you can leave it out. Simmer for 2 hours so all the flavors can meld. Serve with salad and corn bread.

CHICKEN N DUMPLINGS

I like to make this dish on a cold and rainy Sunday. Such a great comfort food!

~ 1 chicken (about 3 pounds), cut up or buy it already cut up
~ 3/4 cup all-purpose flour
~ 1/2 teaspoon each salt & pepper
~ 2 tablespoons olive oil
~ 1 large onion, chopped
~ 2 medium carrots, chopped
~ 2 celery ribs, chopped
~ minced garlic to taste
~ 6 cups chicken stock
~ 1/2 cup white wine – Wine makes if FINE!
~ 2 bay leaves
~ 5 whole peppercorns
~ 1/2 cup heavy whipping cream
~ 2 pinches of minced fresh italian parsley
~ 2 pinches of minced fresh thyme
~ salt and pepper to taste

DUMPLINGS
~ 1-1/3 cups all-purpose flour
~ 2 teaspoons baking powder
~ 3/4 teaspoon salt
~ 2/3 cup milk
~ 1 tbsp butter, melted

In a large Ziploc bag, mix 1/2 cup flour, salt and pepper. Add chicken and shake well to coat. Remove from bag and set aside. In a large stockpot heat olive oil over medium-high heat. Brown chicken on all sides until golden. Remove chicken from pan and add onion, carrots, celery and cook until the onions are tender. Add garlic and stir to mix in with the others. Next, Stir in 1/4 cup flour until blended. Gradually add stock, stirring constantly. Stir in wine, sugar, bay leaves and peppercorns. Return chicken to pan. Bring it back to a boil. Reduce heat, cover and simmer for about 20-25 minutes or until chicken juices run clear. Time for the dumplings, Dumplin'. Whisk flour, baking powder and salt in a bowl. In another bowl, whisk milk and melted butter together. Add to flour mixture and stir until just moistened (do not overmix). Drop by rounded tablespoonfuls onto a parchment paper-lined baking sheet and set aside. Remove chicken from stockpot; cool slightly. Discard bay leaves and skim fat off the top. Remove skin and bones from chicken using two forks, coarsely shred meat into 1- to 1-1/2-in. pieces and return to stock pot. Cook, covered, on high until mixture reaches a simmer. Drop dumplings on top of simmering soup being sure not to overcrowd the pot. Reduce heat to low. Cover pot and cook for another 15-18 minutes or until a toothpick inserted in center of dumplings comes out clean. It is very important not to lift the cover while simmering. The dumplings won't rise properly if you do and who wants flat dumplings??? Certainly not ME. Next, gently stir in cream, parsley and thyme. Season with additional salt and pepper to taste. Serve it up in a large soup bowls… So comforting.

SPICY BOURBON BBQ CHICKEN WINGS

These are the best wings you'll ever have. Soon you will forget all about the buffalo ones ☺ The Bourbon in the marinade and grilling over Mesquite charcoal make these guys so so so very good.

~ 2 pounds chicken wings – get them at the butcher all cut up

~ 1 bottle bullseye original BBQ sauce

~ 1 bottle bullseye hickory smoke BBQ sauce

~ 1 small red onion chopped up

~ 1 cup bourbon

~ a good amount of minced garlic

~ 2 tablespoons honey

~ siracha hot sauce to your taste

Combine the sauce, mix well. Add in chicken wings in a gallon Ziploc bag. Pour in sauce. Make sure all the wings are coated, Take extra air out of the bag and seal. Please in the fridge for 24 to 48 hours to absorb all the goodness. I prefer to BBQ these over mesquite, but you can cook them in the oven at 325 degrees for about 45 minutes. The secret to these is when you BBQ them is to baste them with the leftover BBQ sauce until it's all gone. The BBQ wings will have a crunchie outside skin that has caramelized as you grill them. Once the sauce is all gone the wings are done. Serve on a platter and dig in. Goes well with french potato salad or the mediterranean pasta salad. GREAT PICNIC FARE!

CHEESY CHICKEN BROCCOLI POT PIE

This is so much better than anything you get in the freezer section of your local market. You can also get smaller pie tins and make individual ones.

~ pre-made pie crust, you will need a bottom and a top
~ 2 boneless, skinless chicken breasts
~ 3 tablespoons butter
~ 1 red potato cut into bite size pieces
~ 2 stalks celery - diced
~ 1 carrot – diced
~ 1 red onion, chopped
~ 1 bag white mushrooms
~ 1 head broccoli cut into bite size bits
~ 1 can cheddar cheese soup
~ 1 medium block tillamook extra sharp cheddar cheese
~ 1 egg white whisked with a little water (for top of pie)
~ salt and lemon pepper to taste

Preheat oven to 350. Dice the chicken in to bite size pieces and in a sauté pan add olive oil and brown the chicken until just brown. Remove and put in a large mixing bowl. In a medium pot boil water with some salt and par boil the potato bites. Remove them when just tender but not still crunchy and definitely not mushy. The rest of the cooking will happen when the pie is in the oven. Remove from pan and add to mixing bowl with chicken. In the same pan add 3 tablespoons butter and sauté the onion, celery and mushrooms until they cook down. When they are done remove and add to chicken/potato mix. In the same pan add olive oil and stir fry the broccoli bits until tender but still have a little crunch to them. You can add them to the mix and stir well to mix everything together. Next up is the cheese sauce. In a small saucepan add soup, can of milk and heat to simmering. While that is happening, you should grate the Tillamook cheese. Once the cheese soup is simmering add the shredded cheese and stir until melted. Add that to the chicken filling mixture

and mix well. Let it cool for about 20 minutes or you will melt the pie crust. Now that you have everything ready it's time to assemble! Take your pie plate and line it with one of the pie crusts. Add the chicken cheesy filling to the pie plate. Now it's time to add the pie crust top and crimp the edges. Be sure to make vents in the top to give the steam a place to escape. Brush top with egg whitewash. Sprinkle with lemon pepper. Place pie on a baking sheet and bake for about an hour or until it's brown and you can smell it! Once pie is done let it rest on a wire rack for about 15 minutes before slicing. It is a wonderful oozy slice of heaven. No need for a side dish as this pie has it all going ON!

CHICKEN PICATTA

I'm a huge fan of chicken with lemon so this is my version of veal picatta that is healthy and cost effective. Oh, and yummy too!!!

~ 4 boneless skinless chicken breasts pounded flat

~ olive oil

~ flour

~ fresh lemon juice

~ capers

~ salt & pepper to taste

PICATTA SAUCE

~ 1/4 cup butter

~ 1 1/2 tablespoons flour

~ 1 cup chicken broth

~ juice of 1 lemon, more if you want it really tangy MORE FOR ME!!!

~ 1/2 cup white wine or chicken stock (I prefer WINE!)

~ 3 tablespoons capers drained

~ 2 tablespoons fresh italian parsley chopped

Combine the flour, lemon zest, salt and pepper. Dredge the chicken in flour mixture. Heat olive oil over medium high heat and cook chicken about 4-5 minutes per side or until just until cooked through. Cook in batches if you cannot fit into pan. Remove from pan and place in a dish to keep warm. In the same pan, melt 1/4 cup butter and add flour to create a roux. Whisk until smooth. Cook 1-2 minutes. Gradually stir in chicken broth whisking after each addition until smooth. Add lemon juice, white wine and capers. Simmer 3 minutes, whisking occasionally. Add chicken back to pan and simmer 2-3 minutes. Stir in parsley and serve alone or over pasta.

CHEESY CHICKEN ENCHILADA'S

This is a great dish for a large group. My whole family just loves it!

I don't know how to make it smaller. It's also great for lunch leftovers!

~ 2 tbsp olive oil (or olive oil)

~ 1 small white onion, peeled and diced

~ 4 cooked boneless skinless chicken breasts, shredded

~ 1 (15-ounce) can black beans, rinsed and drained

~ 8 - 10 large flour tortillas (depends on the size of your pan)

~ 2 bags Mexican-blend shredded cheese

~ 2 cans red enchilada sauce (1 for the filling and 1 for covering them)

~ salt and pepper to taste

~ optional toppings: fresh cilantro, chopped red onions, diced avocado, avocado, sour cream, and/ or crumbled cotija cheese

Preheat oven to 350. In large sauté pan, heat oil over medium-high heat. Add onion and sauté for 3 minutes, stirring occasionally. Add shredded chicken and season with a generous pinch of salt and pepper. Sauté the mixture for a few minutes, stirring occasionally. Add in the beans, 1 can enchilada sauce and 1 bag of cheese and stir until evenly combined. Remove pan from heat and set aside. Cover the bottom of your 9 x 13-inch baking dish with a layer of enchilada sauce (this is where the second can comes in) Place about 2 -3 tablespoons of the chicken enchilada mixture down the middle of each tortilla and roll up and nestle them in your baking dish. When they are all comfortable in the dish spread any remaining sauce evenly over the top of the enchiladas, followed by the 2nd bag of cheese. Bake uncovered for 20 minutes, until the enchiladas are cooked through and the tortillas are slightly crispy on the outside. Remove pan from the oven and serve the enchiladas while they're nice and warm, garnished with lots of toppings.

ROAST CHICKEN OR TURKEY BRINE
Makes for a very moist yummy bird!
~ 5 to 6-pound bird. Double recipe of a large Turkey
~ 1 cup cranberry lemonade
~ 1 cup white wine
~ 1 cup brown sugar
~ lots of minced garlic
~ 3 bay leaves
~ 1 cup kosher salt
~ 3 large navel oranges quartered
~ 2 lemons quarters
~ peppercorns
~ italian parsley
~ 2 bags of ice
~ 1 stick of butter
~ 1 large brining bag or larger pot that will fit the bird

Preheat oven to 375. In a large stock pot combine all ingredients. Be sure to squeeze the oranges & lemons to release their juice. Bring to a boil until the sugar has dissolved. Let simmer for 20 minutes. Remove from heat and add ice to cool. When completely cold add the rinsed bird. Or put into a brining bag. Be sure you remove the giblet packet! Cover and place in fridge for at least 24 hours. I usually will go more like 36 to 48. Remove bird from brine and rinse and pat dry. You can discard the brine. Its job is done! Place chicken or turkey on a roasting rack in a roasting pan breast side down and roast for about an hour. Remove from oven and flip the bird. Rub the breast side with the stick of butter and return to oven and cook until done. Usually about 2 hours or 20 mins per pound is the general rule of thumb. You can continue to baste with butter about every 20 minutes if you desire. When done let it rest for 20 minutes before slicing. Serve with cheesy garlic smashed potatoes and fuji apple salad.

TURKEY IN PUFF PASTRY WITH HOMEMADE STUFFING AND BOURBON ORANGE CRANBERRY SAUCE

Let's get Saucy!!!! This is really great with my Turkey in Puff Pastry!

BOURBON ORANGE CRANBERRY SAUCE

~ 1 bag fresh cranberries

~ 1 large navel orange cut in quarters

~ 1 cup water

~ 1 cup sugar

~ ½ cup bourbon

Put all ingredients expect the orange in a saucepan. Squeeze juice from orange and put orange quarters in the saucepan and bring to a boil. Once it begins to boil and the cranberries start to POP reduce heat and simmer for 5 minutes. Remove orange quarters and continue to simmer until the sauce thickens. Remove from heat, set aside and let it cool. You will serve this with the turkey puff pastry.

TURKEY IN PUFF PASTRY

This is my version of Thanksgiving dinner. I'm not sure if I will ever cook another full-size turkey again. These are so YUMMY in your TUMMY!

~ 2 boxes frozen puff pastry sheets (2 sheets per box) put in fridge to thaw
~ fresh turkey breast or turkey cutlets
~ 1-pound italian seasoned ground turkey
~ 1 bunch celery
~ 1 red inion
~ 1 bag sliced white mushrooms
~ 1 tablespoons poultry seasoning mix
~ Salt and pepper to taste
~ 1 cup chopped walnuts
~ 1 cup dried cranberries
~ 1 granny smith apple, cored peeled and cut into bite size pieces
~ chicken stock
~ stuffing mix (I make my own, but you can buy the box stuffing)
~ 2 sticks butter

Chop up celery & onion. In a large pot melt butter and add celery, onion, mushrooms, poultry seasoning, salt & pepper to taste. Cook down until the onion and celery are soft but still have a little crunch to them. Cut up the turkey into bite size pieces and in another sauté pan add olive oil and sauté the turkey until almost done. Don't overcook it or it will be tough. Remove from pan to cool. In the same pan add more olive oil and brown the ground turkey. Once done remove from heat to cool with the other turkey. In a large bowl add the stuffing mix, veggie mix, turkey, walnuts, cranberries and apple. Mix well. Add chicken stock as needed to make the stuffing mix hold together. This will need to chill overnight.

Preheat oven to 450. Take the puff pastry out of the fridge and remove from packaging. Unfold and roll them out a bit. Cut each sheet into 4 squares. You can roll them out a bit but not too much because you will take a "puff" out of the puff pastry. Take a good size spoonful of the stuffing mix and put in the center of each square. Brush the edges with a little water. Pull all 4 corners up over the stuffing and crimp at the top to seal the puff pastry package. Continue this process with the other squares. In a baking dish put a layer of olive oil in the bottom and then place the puff pastry packets in the dish. Bake in oven for about 20 minutes or until they have puffed and are brown or you can smell them. Serve with Bourbon Cranberry Sauce. Wha La. Thanksgiving dinner without the hassle of cooking a big bird! You're Welcome ☺ If you want to freeze them go ahead however when you are ready to heat them up, thaw them completely and heat them slowly in the oven. The puff pastry does not play well with the microwave and you will ruin a wonderful delicious meal and be sad that you didn't listen to me.

DORY'S CHICKEN

My Mom started making this when I was a kid and even though when you hear what the ingredients are you wouldn't think that it would taste good, but it REALLY DOES. So, in honor of my mother Dory I am including it for you all to try. Let me know how you like it!

~ 8 chicken thighs with bone & skin
~ 1 jar of apricot jam
~ 1 bottle of french dressing
~ 2 packet lipton onion soup

Wash and pat dry the chicken. Place in a baking dish skin side up. Pre heat oven to 325. First spoon apricot jam onto each thigh and spread evenly. Next drizzle French dressing over all the thighs and final step is to take the Lipton onion soup packet and shake it up, open it and sprinkle the dry soup mix all over the thighs. That's it. Pop them in the oven for about an hour or until you start to smell them, and they are golden brown. Serve with spicy stir fry broccoli. YUM!

CHICKEN PARM

Another Kela favorite. I am teaching her how to make this so she can make it for her boyfriend Frank who is another fan of my cooking.

~ 2-3 large boneless skinless chicken breasts cut horizontally to make 4 -6 filets depending on how many you are serving

~ 2 large eggs

~ minced garlic to taste

~ fresh italian parsley, chopped

~ salt & pepper to taste

~ 1 cup panko breadcrumbs

~ ½ cup garlic italian breadcrumbs

~ ½ cup fresh grated parmesan cheese

~ ½ cup olive oil for frying

~ 8 oz shredded mozzarella cheese

~ 1/3 cup fresh grated parmesan cheese

~ fresh chopped italian parsley & fresh basil

~ 1 – 2 jars marinara sauce

Preheat oven to 400. Lightly grease a baking dish with non-stick cooking spray. Whisk together eggs, garlic, parsley, salt and pepper in shallow dish. Add chicken breasts into the egg mixture coating evenly. Cover with plastic wrap and marinade for about 30 minutes. Mix breadcrumbs and parmesan cheese in another shallow bowl, mix well. Heat oil up in large skillet. Dip the chicken in the breadcrumb mixture and when the oil is hot and shimmering you can add the chicken and fry until golden brown on both sides. When you are finished browning the chicken you will place it in the prepared baking dish top each breast with sauce, then top with mozzarella and some parmesan too. Bake for about 15-20 minutes or until the cheese is bubbling and getting a little brown. You can serve it as is or over your favorite pasta. I would recommend the fuji apple salad with this dish.

OINK...
Little piggy wants more!

BBQ RIBS
~ 2 slabs extra meaty Safeway brand pork ribs
~ 1 bottle of Bullseye original BBQ sauce
~ 1 bottle of Bullseye honey hickory BBQ sauce
~ minced garlic to taste
~ 1 medium red onion diced
~ fresh cracked black pepper to taste

Rinse ribs and cut slabs into 3 rib sections pierce each section several times with a fork. You should get 4 sections per slab. In a large plastic storage bin that has a sealing top put the BBQ sauce, garlic and onion together. Shake to mix well. Add rib sections and coat with BBQ mixture. Place top on container and seal. Next take the container and shake the ribs with the BBQ sauce for several minutes. Set the container aside and let it marinate for 30 minutes to 1 hour. You can fire up the grill or you can slow cook then in the oven. I prefer the slow oven as they come out juicy and tender.

If using the oven set your temp to 250 - 275 degrees. Put the ribs in a large roasting pan so that they aren't overlapping, rib side down and go low and slow for at least 2 to 3 hours. Be sure to turn them over after the first hour or so and baste with more sauce. Continue cooking until the meat starts to pull back from the rib. Keep basting until the sauce has been absorbed by the meat. I tell you these are the best ribs you will ever eat!!!

CHESSY HAM & POTATO BAKE
Great dish for leftover Honey Baked Ham

~ left over honey baked ham cut into bite size pieces
~ 6 to 8 large whatever type of potato you want to use, sliced very thin
~ 1 red onion slice very thin
~ 2 cans cheddar cheese soup
~ milk
~ large block of tillamook extra sharp cheddar cheese, shredded

CHEESE SAUCE
In a medium saucepan put the 2 cans of cheddar cheese soup and 1 can of milk. Mix will. Keep on low heat until it's simmering. Add shredded cheese and mix well. Keep on low heat, stirring occasionally while you get the ham and potato casserole ready.

HAM, POTATO & ONION CASSEROLE
Preheat oven to 350. In a deep baking dish layer the potato, ham and onions and cheese sauce until the pan is full. Once you have incorporated all the potato/ham/onion /cheese sauce it's OVEN TIME! Place the casserole on a foil lined baking sheet. This will catch any bubbling over of the cheese sauce and keep it from landing on the bottom of your oven and makes for an easy clean up. Place the casserole in the middle of the oven and let it bake for an hour. Then get ready for some cheesy ham and potato yumminess!

STUFFED PORK LOIN ROAST WRAPPED WITH BACON

Pork on Pork Baby! This is a really great dish for a dinner party as the presentation is awesome!

~ 5-pound pork loin roast – butterflied

~ stuffing mix homemade or store bought – your call

~ veggie broth

~ ½ stick of butter

~ 2 stalks celery

~ 2 shallots

~ 1 bag white mushrooms

~ baby spinach leaves

~ 1-pound bacon

~salt and pepper to taste

~ toothpicks

~ kitchen string to tie the roast

Preheat oven to 350. Butterfly pork loin and pound with mallet to make a flat consistent thickness. Salt and pepper the roast. Finely chop the celery, shallots & mushrooms. In a sauté pan melt the butter and add the chopped veggies. Cook down until softened. Add veggies to stuffing mix. Add veggie broth as needed to bring the stuffing mix together but not soggy. Mix well. Take the stuffing and layer it on top of the butterflied pork loin roast making sure that the stuffing layer is even. Add

a layer of baby spinach leaves. Next comes the roll up. Start on the smaller side and roll it up until you reach the larger side. Use toothpicks to secure while you get your string ready. Slide it under the roast and tie it together every couple of inches. Remove toothpicks when you are done. Place the roast on a rack in a roasting pan. Bacon is next on deck. I like to do a basket weave pattern because I think that's what makes it a special presentation. Just start laying strips going one direction and the other strips get woven in the opposite direction. Once that is complete is oven time! Roast for 20 minutes per pound making sure that the bacon is cooked and is nice and brown and bacony!

BAAAAA...

BUTTERFLIED BBQ'D LEG OF LAMB

Best way to have lamb!

~ 1 small leg of lamb butterflied off the bone

~ minced garlic to taste

~ olive oil

~ salt & pepper

~ rosemary sprigs

~ oregano

~ italian parsley

~ mesquite charcoal

Butterfly leg of lamb, if you don't know how to do this you can have your butcher do it for you. Lay it flat and pound it out to make it an even thickness. Salt and pepper both sides. Combine the garlic, herbs and olive oil into a paste. Rub it all over the lamb. Place on a baking sheet, cover with plastic wrap and let it rest in the fridge for at least an hour. I prefer to let it sit overnight but that's just how I roll! Time to fire up the Barbie!! Make sure the coals have burned down as this will be a very HOT fire. When the coals are ready place the fat side down first to get the grill marks. Let that cook for about 5 minutes or until that side looks done. If you are a BBQer you will know what I'm talking about. When it's time, flip it

and cook the other side. Make sure it is cooked through, you make want to check the temp with a thermometer. It should be medium rare. I have been doing this for so long I just know when it's done. Remove from BBQ and let it rest for 20 minutes before slicing. Serve with mediterranean pasta salad or whatever side or salad you prefer.

GLUB, GLUB, GLUB

GRILLED SWORDFISH
My absolute favorite fish YUM!!!
~ 2 1/2 pound swordfish steaks
~ 1/2 c extra virgin olive oil
~ 2 fresh lemons
~ minced garlic to taste
~ 1/2 cup chopped italian parsley
~ salt & pepper to taste

In a shallow baking dish mix olive oil, lemon juice, garlic & parsley. Stir well. Add fish. Coat fish with marinade. Cover and let sit in fridge for at least 30 minutes. Fire up the BBQ and grill to perfection. Serve with lemon wedges and cold coos coos veggie salad.

GRILLED JUMBO PRAWNS
These are great for as an appetizer served cold with a lemon vinaigrette or as the star of your next dinner party or as an added quest to your bloody mary!
~ 2 pounds raw JUMBO prawns, deveined & peeled
~ marinade from the grilled swordfish recipe

Follow the directions as you did for the swordfish. There will be one more step as you will need to skewer the prawns before you grill them. Use 2 metal skewers one for each end of the prawns so they have better support and are easier to flip with your tongs. Put as many prawns as you can on each. Fire up the barbie and grill. Serve with grilled veggies and fuji apple salad.

PRAWN SCAMPI WITH BROCCOLI & LINGUINE

This is another favorite because it has LEMON!!!

~ 1 package fresh linguini

~ 1 head of fresh broccoli cut into florets

~ olive oil

~ 1-pound large prawns, peeled and deveined

~ 6 tablespoons butter

~ minced garlic to taste

~ red pepper flake to taste

~ zest & juice of 1 lemon…You know I'm gonna use more!

~ 1 slices lemon for garnish

~ salt & lemon pepper to taste

In a large pot bring salted water to a boil. Heat a large skillet to medium high heat add olive oil, add prawns and cook on each side until opaque. Remove prawns from pan and place on a plate and cover with plastic wrap to keep them warm. Next up, back to the same pan you will melt the butter and add a tablespoon more olive oil, garlic and red pepper flake, sauté until the garlic starts to get brown. At this point you add the broccoli florets and until they are al dente. Toss back in the shrimp. Squeeze the lemon juice over everything. I use 2 lemons because I can, add zest and Italian parsley. Garnish with lemon slices. Yes, you will need another lemon for that! Haha! Serve immediately while it's hot! No need for a side dish, this is a one dish wonder!

GRILLED SALMON

A very dear friend turned ne onto this cooking method. It's so easy and the fish comes out perfect every time! I won't cook salmon any other way! Super simple

~ salmon filet with skin, size will depend on how many you are serving

~ ranch salad dressing

~ lemon pepper & salt to taste

~ lemon wedges

~ aluminum foil

You can BBQ this or bake it in the oven. Make a tray for the salmon out of aluminum foil put it on a baking sheet. Place fish skin side down on foil. Slather ranch dressing all over the meat side of the fish. Add salt & lemon pepper on top of dressing. If you are baking this in the oven you should preheat the oven to 350. Bake in oven for about 25 minutes or until the fish is firm. Remove from oven and let it rest for about 10 minutes. If

BBQing (I prefer this method using mesquite. It adds a smoky flavor to the fish. Fire up the barbie and wait for the coals to be ready. Place the foil tray on the grill and cover with lid for about 10 minutes or until the edges of the fish are bubbling and are starting to get crispy. This method will cook faster as the coals will be hotter than the oven method. To remove the fish from the tray, use a large spatula and slide it over the skin and under the meat. The skin will stay on the foil tray and you will lift off a beautifully cooked moist piece of fish. Clean up is a snap as all you do is throw away the foil tray skin and all. Serve with spicy stir fry broccoli or grilled lemon pepper corn.

YOU WANT FRIES WITH THAT?

SMASHED POTATOES WITH GARLIC AND ASIAGO CHEESE
In my opinion, this is the only way to make mashed potatoes
~ 6 medium size red potatoes
~ minced garlic to taste
~ 4 tablespoons butter
~ 1 cup sour cream
~2 bags asiago cheese (1 goes into the smash and 1 for on top)
~salt and pepper to taste

Cut up potatoes leaving the skins on. In a large pot with salted water turn on high heat and bring to a boil. Add potatoes and cook until barely fork tender. Drain potatoes and put in a stand mixer, add butter and garlic and beat slowly until the butter melts do not beat them on high as you want to keep some chucks as you will be finishing this in the oven. Add sour cream and 1 bag of cheese and mix well. Add salt and pepper to taste. Take from blender and turn out into a baking dish and spread it out and top with the other bag of cheese. Bake in a 350 oven for about 30 minutes or until the cheese is all melty and bubbly. Goes great with any dish, delish!

SPICY STIR FRY BROCCOLI
~ 2 heads of broccoli, cut into little bite size florets
~ 2 lemons
~ olive oil
~ soy sauce
~ crushed red chili flakes

In a WOK or large pan put a fair amount of olive oil and turn up the heat to high. Cut lemons in half. Once the pan is smoking hot add the broccoli and stir fry for a couple of minutes. This is a fast dish so stay alert. Squeeze lemon juice into the pan and continue to toss. Add a splash or two of soy sauce and the red chili flakes and cook until tender yet still has it's crunch! There you have it. Easy peasy! I like this with my grilled salmon or swordfish.

CHEESY GARLIC BREAD

this is a fun one that EVERYBODY likes! Goes great with my lasagna or any pasta dish or it stand on its own as well.

~ 2 large loafs of crusty sourdough bread

~ 4 sticks of butter

~ lots of minced garlic

~CHEESE, CHEESE and more CHEESE – Use whatever you like. I use mozzarella, extra sharp cheddar, asiago, jack and whatever else strikes my fancy at the time.

Cut the loafs in half and place on baking sheets. Preheat oven to 375. Partially soften butter in microwave safe bowl. You will be making a butter garlic paste. Add garlic and whisk them together. If the butter melted too much, then put it in the fridge to set up a little more. Next you spread the butter garlic paste all over the cut side up for both loafs. Use all the butter mixture, you'll be happy that you did. Combine all cheeses in a large bowl and then top all the bread with all that cheese until the bowl is empty and it's all on the bread halves. Put the baking sheets into the oven and wait for them to get all bubbly and golden brown. Once the bread has cooled a bit you can slice into individual pieces. Once you taste this, you'll never have any other type of garlic bread!

LEMON PEPPER GRILLED CORN

Super simple and oh so good, I'll never use butter again!!!

~ 2 ears of shucked corn

~ lemon olive oil

~ salt

~ lemon pepper

Rub ears with lemon olive oil. Sprinkle with salt & lemon pepper and coat the entire ear of corn, then just grill until it is a little charred. Serve with anything!

HOMEMADE CHEESY CROUTONS - MAKES A GREAT SNACK!

My kids just love these as 1 snack. I also us then as my stuffing mix. The asiago cheese adds a unique flavor,

~ 2 sliced loaves for asiago sour dough bread that you can get at Molly Stones cut into cubes

~ 1 bunch italian parsley- chopped

~ lots of minced garlic

~ 2 sticks melted butter

~ salt and pepper

Preheat oven to 350. In a large roasting pan add all the cubed bread and spread out. Sprinkle chopped parsley and minced garlic evenly over the bread cubes. Next take the melted butter and drizzle over all the bread and stir so the bread is coated with the butter, herb and garlic then pop it in the oven. You should toss the mixture about every 2 minutes to be sure that the bread toasts evenly. Check for doneness. When they crunch they are done. Remove from oven to cool and store in ziploc bags until needed.

These are so super simple to make. Store bought just won't cut it anymore.

SHOW ME THE GOODIES!!

YUMMY YUM!

GINGERED APPLES IN PUFF PASTRY

My version of apple pie - individual pillows of joy!!! Can you tell that I love using puff pastry?

~ 2 granny smith apples

~ 2 fuji apples

~ ½ cup light brown sugar

~ ½ cup dark brown sugar

~ 1 tablespoon cinnamon

~ 1 teaspoon ground ginger

~ 1 teaspoon ground nutmeg

~ juice of one lemon

~ 3 tablespoons cream of tartar

~ 4 tablespoons butter

~ 1 package frozen puff pastry sheets (2)

Preheat oven to 450. In a large saucepan melt the butter. Core, peel and slice apples. Add apples, sugar, spices and lemon juice into the butter mixture. Next add cream of tartar, mix well. Cook until the apples are soft but not mushy and the sugar has melted. Remove from heat and let cool before putting in the puff pastry. Lay out puff pastry sheets and cut into 4 squares. You should have 8 total all together. Place the cooled filling in the middle of the squares and brush the edges with water. Next pull the corners up and pinch together just like you did for the chicken and turkey in puff pastry. Place on a baking sheet and bake at 450 for 15 minutes or until the pastry has puffed and is golden brown. Serve with french vanilla ice cream.

KELA'S PUMPKIN PIE

This one is easy too except you have to grow your own pumpkins and then cook and puree the flesh to get your pumpkin puree. I do this every year because she asks me to. She loves watching the pumpkin grow as she knows it will be for her special pie. Once you have the puree you can follow any pumpkin pie recipe to achieve your results.

~ 1 1/2 cups fresh pumpkin puree, the key here is FRESH!

~ 1 can evaporated milk

~ 2 eggs

~ brown sugar

~ cinnamon
~ nutmeg
~ ground cloves
~ ground ginger
~ single crust pie shell

Preheat oven to 375. Make the pie shell either store bought or homemade, your choice. Blend fresh puree with all other ingredients and pour into pie shell. Bake for about an hour or until it is set in the middle. Cool before serving with cinnamon whipped cream. YUM!

BLENDER CHEESE CAKE
This is another easy one and is just so good especially in the summer when you can add all kinds of fresh fruit.

CRUST
~ 1 package honey graham crackers, crushed
~ 1 cup brown sugar
~ 1 stick melted butter

Preheat oven to 350. Mix the crushed graham crackers with the brown sugar, add the melted butter. While still warm press the mixture into the bottom and sides of your buttered 9"spring form pan. Put crust in oven and bake for about 20 minutes. Take it out and let it cool completely before adding the filling.

FILLING
Love this because all you do is put the ingredients into a blender and blend until smooth.
~ 2 16oz packages cream cheese - cut into 1" cubes
~ 1 container sour cream
~ 2 eggs
~ 1 cup sugar

~ zest and juice from 1 lemon and 1 orange

Preheat oven to 375. Start with the sour cream and blend until smooth. Add the eggs and sugar and blend until smooth again. Add citrus, blend until smooth. While the blender is running slowly add the cream cheese and make sure the mixture is smooth before adding any more cubes. When all the cubes have been added blend on high for about a minute. Pour your cream cheese mixture into your prepared crust and bake for about an hour or until set in the middle. Cool completely before serving. Top with summer fruit to add additional flavor. Try strawberries, blueberries, mixed berries, mandarin oranges, grapefruit segments, kiwi slices, LEMON Haha!...The possibilities are endless! I once made cantaloupe cheesecake and it was quite good. Let your imagination run wild.

OH SO EASY STRAWBERRY ANGEL FOOD CAKE
My family just loves this one!
~ 1 store bought angle food cake
~ 1 large basket fresh strawberries
~ 2 - 3 tablespoons bakers sugar
~ 1 - 2 oz grand mariner - optional
~ 1 carton bavarian whipping cream
~ 1 teaspoon vanilla

Take the angle food cake and slice it so you have 3 layers. Set aside. Clean the strawberries and slice them. Sprinkle with sugar (and Grand mariner if you choose), set aside. Next whip the bavarian whipping cream and vanilla until you have stiff whipped cream. Put a layer of angle-food cake on a serving platter. Spread a layer of whipped cream then put a layer of strawberries. Add a little more whipped cream and then another layer of angle-food cake. Continue this process until the cake is complete. Top with remaining strawberries and there you go. 4th of July option would be to add blueberries and little star cookies with sparklers.

CHOCOLATE WALNUT BROWNIES TOPPED WITH FRENCH VANILLA ICE CREAM & BRANDIED CHERRIES

~ 1 box your favorite brownie mix
~ 1 cup chopped walnuts
~ 3"- 4" round individual pie tins (need 5)
~ 1 can bing cherries
~ 1 cup good brandy
~ 2 tablespoons baker sugar
~ french vanilla ice cream

Make brownies per the instructions on the box. Pour into buttered individual pie tins. Bake according to directions. Put canned cherries in a sauce pan. Add brandy & sugar and heat for 10 minutes to combine flavors. Plate individual brownies, top with a scoop of french vanilla ice cream and top with hot brandied cherry topping.

PUMPKIN SCONES WITH CINNAMON ICING

Another Kela suggestion that I created from our fresh pumpkin puree
~ 2 cups all-purpose flour
~ 1/3 cup brown sugar
~ 1 teaspoon baking powder
~ 1/2 teaspoon baking soda
~ 1/2 teaspoon kosher salt
~ 1 teaspoon ground cinnamon
~ 3/4 teaspoon ground ginger

~ 3/4 teaspoon ground cloves
~ 1/2 teaspoon ground nutmeg
~ 1 stick cold butter
~ 1/2 cup pumpkin puree, again FRESH is best!
~ 1 tablespoon molasses
~ 3 tablespoons half and half or cream
~ 1 large egg
~ 2 teaspoons vanilla extract

SIMPLE SUGAR GLAZE

~ 1 cup powdered sugar, sifted
~ 1 to 2 tablespoons half and half or heavy cream

PUMPKIN SPICE GLAZE

~ 1 cup powdered sugar, sifted
~ 1 tablespoon pumpkin puree - remember FRESH!
~ 1/8 teaspoon cloves
~ 1/8 teaspoon ground nutmeg
~ 1/8 teaspoon ground ginger
~ 1/4 teaspoon ground cinnamon
~ 1 to 2 tablespoons half and half or heavy cream

Center a rack in the middle of the oven and preheat to 400. Line a baking sheet with parchment paper or use non-stick cooking spray. Whisk the flour, sugar, baking powder, baking soda, salt, cinnamon, ginger, cloves and nutmeg together until blended. Cut the butter into small cubes then scatter over the flour mixture. Use two knives or a pastry cutter to "cut" the butter into the flour until the mixture resembles coarse cornmeal with a few pea-sized bits of butter, about 5 minutes. (You could also use a food processor for this – if using, add flour mixture to the bowl of a food processor, add the cold butter cubes. Then pulse three to four times until the mixture looks like coarse cornmeal or crumbs). In a separate bowl, whisk the pumpkin puree, molasses, half and half, egg and vanilla extract until blended. Stir the pumpkin mixture into the flour and butter mixture until a soft dough forms. Transfer the dough to a floured surface. Knead three to four times until it comes together. Roll out the dough into a 10-inch by 7-inch rectangle You can use a cookie cutter like I did in the picture or for a more traditional scone shape you can cut the rectangle in half lengthwise then cut into 4 even pieces crosswise, making eight rectangles. Cut each rectangle into two triangles, making 16 scones. Transfer scones to the baking sheet then bake 10 to 15 minutes or until golden brown and a toothpick inserted into the middle comes out clean. Transfer to a wire rack and cool completely. For the simple sugar glaze, add the sugar to a medium bowl then add one tablespoon of half and half. Mix together until smooth but not too thin. If when you dip a spoon into the glaze and lift it up it should slowly drizzle back into the glaze, it is fine. If it is too thick, add a little more half and half (a little goes a long way, here). If it is too thin, add a little more powdered sugar. In another bowl, make the pumpkin spice glaze. Combine the sugar, pumpkin puree, spices and add one tablespoon of half and half. Stir and check consistency. Adjust the same way as you would the simple glaze. Dip each cooled scone directly into the simple sugar glaze then place glazed side up back onto the cooling rack. Use a spoon to drizzle a zigzag pattern of the pumpkin spice glaze across each scone. Wait 15 minutes or until the glaze has set then enjoy! To store baked and glazed scones cover with plastic wrap. We recommend storing in the refrigerator if storing them for more than a day. They will lose a little moisture but will still taste great.

ANGEL FOOD CUPCAKES

~ ¾ cup + 2 tablespoons bakers' sugar

~ ½ cup cake flour

~ pinch of salt

~ 6 egg whites at room temperature

~ 1 ½ tablespoons warm water

~ ½ teaspoon vanilla

~ ¾ teaspoon cream of tarter

WHIPPED CREAM CHEESE TOPPING

~ 1 ½ cups heavy whipping cream

~ 6 oz softened cream cheese

~ ½ cup powdered sugar

~ fresh berries, whatever you like or a combination of all

Preheat oven to 350. In a mixing bowl sift together half of the sugar and cake flower, add a pinch of salt. In a stand mixer whisk together egg whites, water, vanilla extract and cream of tartar. Once everything is mixed you can turn up the speed on the mixture and whip the mixture on medium speed and gradually add the remaining sugar a little at a time until it forms soft peaks. Transfer the egg white mixture to a large mixing bowl. Next you will gradually sift just enough flour mixture to cover the peaks and gently fold that into the egg white mixture a little at a time until it is completely incorporated. Line your muffin tins with paper liners. I use the jumbo ones because it makes such a nice presentation. Fill cups almost to the top and bake in your preheated oven for about 18 – 20 minutes. While the cupcakes are baking you will make the topping. Back to the stand mixer and with a clean bowl and whipping attachment you will whip the heavy cream until is forms soft peaks. Set this aside and then whip the cream cheese until light and fluffy. Add whipped cream to the cream cheese mixture along with powdered sugar and whip until soft peaks form. Store in refrigerator until the cupcakes have completely cooled. Frost the cupcakes and top with fruit. I bet you thought I was going to try and sneak in some lemon DUH? Well you can just use lemon extract instead of vanilla and add lemon zest to the frosting and garnish with ½ a lemon slice!

CAN IT!

I discovered the fine art of canning several years ago and it has become an annual event for me. My friends think I'm crazy because this usually happens in the summer when it's 90 degrees outside and I am slaving over a huge canning pot of boiling water. I don't hear them say I'm crazy when I share my efforts with them when I'm done.

SPICY GARLIC DILL PICKLES
Several of my friends go crazy for these pickles

~ 2 to 3 pounds pickling cucumbers

~ 1 1/2 cups apple cider vinegar

~ 1 1/2 cups filtered water

~ 2 tablespoons pickling salt

~ minced garlic

~ dill seed weed

~ black peppercorns

~ 1 teaspoon red chili flakes

~ 4-pint jars or 2-quart jars

To sterilize the jars and lids for canning, place empty jars, lids & rings on a metal rack in a large, 16-qt canning pot. (Jars must rest on a rack in the pot, not on the bottom of the pot). Fill with warm water and bring to a boil. Reduce heat to keep the jars hot and ready for canning. Remove jars from canning bath and set aside. Meanwhile while the jars are bathing, wash and dry pickling cucumbers. Cut into chips, spears or leave whole, depending on your preference. In a medium saucepan combine vinegar, water and bring to a boil. Equally divide minced garlic, dill weed, peppercorns and red chili flakes between the jars. Pack cucumbers into jars as tightly as you can without crushing them. Pour the brine into the jars, leaving 1/4 inch headspace (that's the amount of space between the surface of the brine and the rim of the jar). Remove any air bubbles from jars by gently tapping them. You can also use a wooden chopstick or plastic utensil to help remove stubborn bubbles. Wipe rims and apply lids and bands (don't screw them on too tightly). Lower jars into your canning bath once again. When the water returns to a boil process for about 15 minutes. When time is up, remove jars from canning bath and allow them to cool. When jars are cool enough to handle, the tops should make a "pop" sound. Be sure to check that they all sealed. Let pickles rest for at least one week before eating.

PICKLED ASPARAGUS
This is my dearest friend Nancy's FAVORITE. She goes crazy for it every time I decided to make it. Happy to put a smile on her face!
~ 30 asparagus spears trimmed
~ 1/3 cup kosher salt

- ~ 2 quarts cold water
- ~ 2 cups distilled white vinegar
- ~ 2/3 cup sugar
- ~ 1 teaspoon coarse salt
- ~ 1 teaspoon mustard seed
- ~ 2 teaspoons dill weed
- ~ 1 white onion sliced into rings
- ~ 2 heads garlic separated into whole cloves and peeled
- ~ 1/2 teaspoon chili pepper flakes
- ~ 2 sprigs fresh dill

Trim the cut end of the asparagus spears. Place asparagus in a large bowl with 1/3 cup salt, and cover with water. Let stand in salt water while preparing the brine. In a saucepan over medium heat, combine the vinegar, sugar, 1 teaspoon of salt, mustard seed, dill weed, onion slices and minced garlic. Bring brine mixture to a boil for a couple of minutes. Turn down to a simmer. Drain salted water from asparagus. Next add asparagus to the saucepan with the brine mixture. Simmer for 4-6 minutes until asparagus turns a dull shade of green. Using tongs, remove asparagus from mixture and place in two-pint size wide mouth jars tip side up. Tuck one dill sprig and minced garlic into each jar, and sprinkle in 1/4 teaspoon of red pepper flakes. Pour hot pickling liquid into the jars, filling to within 1/4 inch of the rim. Close the jar with an airtight lid, and place in the refrigerator for at least 3 hours to cool, use within 2 weeks.

BREAD N BUTTER PICKLES

Not everyone likes Bread N Butter pickles, but I sure do and that's all that matters.

~ 2 1/2 pounds pickling cucumbers

~ 1-pound white onions, thinly sliced

~ 1/4 cup kosher salt

~ 1 1/4 cup white distilled vinegar

~ 1 cup apple cider vinegar

~ 2 1/4 cups sugar

~ 1 tablespoon mustard seeds

~ 1 teaspoon crushed red pepper flakes

~ 3/4 teaspoon celery seeds

~ 1-inch cinnamon stick

~ 1 tablespoon ground allspice

~ 6 whole cloves plus a pinch of ground cloves

~ 1/2 teaspoon turmeric

Rinse the cucumbers and cut off 1/8-inch from the ends and discard. Slice the cucumbers in 1/4-inch thick slices, place in a large bowl and add the sliced onions and pickling salt. Stir so that all the salt is well distributed among the slices. Cover with a clean tea towel (thin towel, not terry cloth). Cover with a couple of inches of crushed ice. Put in the refrigerator and let chill for 4 hours. Remove the towel with ice and discard. Rinse the cucumber and onion slices thoroughly, drain. Rinse and drain again. To sterilize the jars and lids for canning, place empty jars, lids & rings on a metal rack in a large, 16-qt canning pot. (Jars must rest on a rack in the pot, not on the bottom of the pot). Fill with warm water and bring to a boil. Reduce heat to keep the jars hot and ready for canning. While you are preparing the jars, you will make the vinegar canning syrup. In a 4 qt or 6 qt pot, place the vinegar, sugar, and all of the spices. Bring to a boil. Once the sugar has dissolved, add the sliced cucumbers and onions. Bring to a boil again. When your syrup is ready you will remove jars & lids from their canning pot with tongs or jar lifters. Place jars/lids on a towel on your counter. As soon as the sugar/vinegar solution begins boiling again, use a slotted spoon to start packing the hot jars with the cucumbers. First pack a jar to an inch from the rim with the vegetables. Then pour hot vinegar sugar syrup over the vegetables to a half inch from the rim. Wipe the rim clean with a paper towel. Place a sterilized lid on the jar. Secure with a metal screw band. Return filled jars to the same canning pot with its already hot water. Water level needs to be at least one inch above the top of the jars. Bring to a boil, cover and let boil hard for 15 minutes. Remove jars from pot. Let cool down to room temperature. Jars should make a popping sound as their lids seal. If a lid doesn't properly seal, do not store the jar outside of the refrigerator. If they do, then put them in your pantry! They will last for about 6 month that is unless you eat them all first. I like to keep them in the fridge so they are crunchy and cold. Great on sandwiches.

NANCY KAY'S BIZILLION VEGGIE MARINARA SAUCE

I make my marinara sauce every Labor Day weekend because it takes 3 days to make it the right way. I "can it" so I have fresh sauce for the entire year and my friends agree it's the best tasting sauce ever! Beats Ragu that's for sure ☺ I go to Segonia's open air market in Redwood City and get every kind of tomato and veggie they have. I just love the whole process of making my Marinara sauce from the shopping, to the prep work, to making the sauce and finally getting it into jars!

~As many tomatoes and veggies that you feel comfortable with. The sky's the limit!
~ lots of minced garlic
~ 2 large cans for Italian crushed tomatoes
~ 1 bunch each of fresh basil, italian parsley and oregano - chopped
~ a bottle of cupcake red velvet red wine
~ 4 packets thick spaghetti sauce mix

First will come the shopping. Use whatever veggies you prefer I'll leave that up to you. Next is prep chopping veggies then in a very large stock pot add olive oil to coat the bottom. Add onion, mushrooms, sweet peppers and sauté until cooked down. Add garlic salt & pepper. The most time-consuming thing about this sauce is peeling the tomatoes. I use a combo of heirloom, roma and beefsteak. Any tomato I can get my hands on goes into my sauce. To peel tomatoes, you will need a pot of boiling water and an ice bath. Take out the stem and with a knife mark the bottom with an X.

Place the tomatoes in boiling water for a few minutes and then drop them into the ice bath. The skin will come right off. Continue with this process until all the tomatoes are peeled. I like to do a rough chop on them and add them to the big pot with the other veggies. I then add the 2 cans of crushed tomatoes and the fresh herbs. Give that a good stir. Add the whole bottle of red wine and stir. Next you will add the thick spaghetti sauce packets dry. Do not add water! The tomatoes already did that for you. Stir well and let it simmer away stirring occasionally so it doesn't burn and stick to the bottom. Remove from stove and let cool. Cover and keep in the fridge overnight. Next day take it out and continue the simmering process. This is when I add in cubed zucchini. Let it simmer away stirring occasionally. Now you should be getting your jars ready. In a canning pot boil water and place jars and lids in the boiling water for 20 minutes, use tongs to remove jars and place on a towel while you get the other ones done. When all the jars are ready it's time to can. Ladle sauce into each jar leaving a ¼ at the top. Put on tops and ring and get them ready for the canning bath. Put jars back in boiling water, cover the pot and let them boil for another 20 minutes. After that time, they are ready to come out. Use your tongs again to remove them and put them back on the towel to cool. You should hear the tops POP. That's when you know that they have properly sealed and once cool can be stored on your pantry for up to a year. Mine never last that long because I give them to friends or use the sauce to make my lasagna ☺ I hope you enjoy this process as much as I do. I look forward to Labor Day week end every year for this reason.

Printed in the United States
By Bookmasters